Words From The River

Poems by
James Dalton Byrd

Vabella Publishing
P.O. Box 1052
Carrollton, Georgia 30112

©Copyright 2013 by James Dalton Byrd

All rights reserved. No part of the book may be reproduced or utilized in any form or by any means without permission in writing from the author. All requests should be addressed to the publisher.

Manufactured in the United States of America

13-digit ISBN 978-1-938230-42-4

Library of Congress Control Number 2013910041

Introduction (A Poem's Way)

Siren Borealis 3
A Poet Speaks 4
Coffee 5
One Step Down 6
Short List 7
An Unfortunate Word 7
Photographs by a balcony window 9
Concerning the Converse of Eagles and Men .. 10
Fish Tale 11
Barnyard Bully 12
For Your Mother and Mine 13
Grandpa 15
Beachcombing 16
Save the Paper 17
Deer River Farewell 18
Grendel's Child 20
Calypso's Children 22
The End of a Song 24
Hero 27
Huey Rider 28
In Green Fields 29
Veterans' Day 30
The Homecoming 32
Damned Strange 33
Huey 34
The Missing one 36
Carnival 37
A Family Album at Christmas 38
Swamp Water 39
Ivy 40
Spirit Walk 42
On Deep River Flow 44
Sing, Wounded Soul 45
Critical Mass 46
Cirque du Soleil 47

Totems 48
Two Women by the Sea 50
Cricket 51
Laws 52
Dawn of a Lesser Light 55
Under the Wizard's Hat 56
Tranquil Summer Memories 57
Winter's Clear Light 58
Words From the River 59
In the Glowing of Fall 60
At Winter's End 61

Haiku 62
Novice
Got it Right
Cycle
Renewal
Essence
Oracles
Winter

Explanations and Inspirations 64

Deer River Flow

Introduction

Originally, I intended to write a book of poems only about Deer River Flow, my friends there, and the surrounding area. I failed. The idea began when a line for a poem came into my mind… "words from the river." So many poems and ideas come to me while I enjoy Deer River in my kayak. I thought I would write a poem about Deer River and give it the title: "Words From the River". But, as it usually works out, those words had their own idea of where they belonged.

Several people have asked me how a poem comes into being or what leads me to write something. An attempt to explain the source of an idea or inspiration will be in a section following the poems in this collection. However, there are some poems that trick the poet into writing them or that take form with no explanation. The poem on the facing page was written as I was substituting for a literature teacher at Central High School of Carroll County. The students were given an assignment to write a poem, so I decided I would write one while they wrote theirs. It seems to lend itself to the object of this introduction.

A Poem's Way

A poem can find its way
with thoughts softly falling.
Nudging words into play,
a soul to souls, calling.

Words drift from dream's realm,
all silently singing.
A poet at the helm
guides each to its meaning.

A poem can rise by force,
from terror, or from dread.
It can take its own course,
demanding to be read.

So great, you know it is,
when, in spite of his pride,
the learned poet is
just along for the ride.

De Bars Mountain from Deer River Flow

Siren Borealis

Come with me…
to where Dianna's Bow last touches De Bars Mountain
and where loons sing of their love.

Come with me…
let the kayaks glide into valleys where legends live
and the great forest hides her secrets 'neath robes of green.

Come with me…
on a quicksilver path across coldwater blue
to where tall trees whisper their primal stories.

Come with me…
and let morning find you drifting in wonder
amid water and trees set ablaze by a rising star.

Come with me…..

A Poet Speaks

She stands before us
to open her heart
so that we are given
new vistas within ourselves.
She becomes vulnerable
to her own words.
Words winding around her,
giving quick flashes
of who she is.
A sacrifice that
makes those words
greater in meaning,
tightening the webs,
and pulling her in
to the soft trap
of herself.

Coffee

Jake, Joe, Java the Hit…
Tar, a cup of road kill…

A good old friend
to a traveler,
to a soldier.
To a preacher
or a whore.

Help on the late shift
for the doctor,
for the nurse.
For the welder
and the cop

Comfort in the cold
for a hunter,
for a farmer,
a fisherman,
or a bum.

Max,
    Grind,
        Liquid road patch…
            A cup of coffee.

One Step Down

Draft beer,

chess boards,

and Kerouac cool.

Cerebral graffiti and
a Robot-in-Drag juke box
bubbling out fifty years of good jazz.

A virtuoso burger flipper
destroying the laws of physics,
making gravity play the fool.

On the restroom walls,
the musings of poets
and philosophers…

overwritten since,
by lesser bards

and now
closed.

Soon to be
apartments.

Short List

Rainy day.
Simple soup.
Good friends.
What more?

An Unfortunate Word

No is such an
unfortunate word.

Opportunities are lost
when it is left
to stand alone.

So many hearts ache
when it rushes out
on solo flight.

It is too short
to explain itself.

Peach

Photographs by a Balcony Window

        A woman sitting
        by a balcony window
        with the man
        whose heart
        she holds.

        A man sitting
        by a balcony window,
        his kind eyes
        showing his love
        for her.

        Their love is sweet
        by the balcony window.
        Peaceful, warm,
        with a golden cat
        playing in the sun.

Concerning the Converse of Eagles and Men

Sometimes I wonder…
what visits the avian brain
of the eagle gracing a branch near the lake.
Is there any thought there?
Is there some strange, birdly insight
delving into the business of fishes?
Or do I merely project my own thoughts
 into those fearsome eyes?
I heard of a fellow here who feeds the eagle.
He holds up a fish and the eagle flies down
and alights on his boat.
Do the man and the eagle speak
in a trans-species tongue?
Do they tell each other of the fish caught
and of those that got away?
Sometimes I wonder…
which is the better liar?

Fish Tale

There is a place between water and sky
known only by my kayak and I.
Where my soul, with a heartfelt sigh,
looks at me straight in the eye.

What it thinks, I am not sure,
for I am not exactly pure.
It knows it must, again, endure
as I affix my fishing lure.

I cast out to see what will bite
in this serene and lovely site.
Then I see a wondrous sight…
a great fish striking with all its might.

The line grows taut and starts to sing.
The mighty fish comes leaping.
The size sets my mind a'reeling,
for of all fish, this fish is king.

It pulled my kayak 'round and 'round.
Then into the deep the fish did sound
to find a log to wrap around
and serve me sorrow without bound.

The line around the log did rake
until the line did sadly break.
Fortune deserted me on that lake
and let the fish my lure to take.

There is a place between water and sky
known only by my kayak and I.
Where my soul, with a heartfelt sigh,
says, "Don't go telling another lie!".

Barnyard Bully

He was a barnyard bully. He was feathered, mean, and wooly.
He squawked all day but he made the hens lay.
He was faster than a bullet and Hell on a pullet.
He was the master of the pens and the idol of the hens.
Now, he could chase a dog and intimidate a hog.
He could make the farmer's wife run for her life.
Then along came a rooster by the name of Leghorn Brewster
who challenged his right to make the sun light.

Well, they crowed and they crowed 'til they was pigeon-toed,
they circled to the right and started to fight.
The feathers flew and confusion grew
'til there was a mighty roar from the kitchen door.
The farmer came out with a holler and a shout
and picked up a stick to end the fight quick.
Our hero fled but Brewster lost his head
'cause he wouldn't give ground to Farmer Brown.

Now, Brewster's through in a rooster stew
And the other got hit with a cataleptic fit.
Need I explain, he's now a weather vane
And everybody knows where the cold wind blows.
Oh, the moral of the story isn't quite so gory.
Every politician better pay close attention.
It's all the same if you simmer in a stew
Or swing with the wind in the public view.

For Your Mother and Mine

We did not know them as the girls they were.
When their dreams were bright
and their paths were paved with hope.

We did not know them as young women;
when they danced through the night…
and their laughter was music.

We did not know them as young brides.
Their eyes shining with pride and love…
walking toward a new life.

We did not know them when they bore us
and through their pain and strength
brought us into this life.

We know them only as our mothers,
vessels of wisdom, tenderness, courage…
and, above all, love.

Galveston, Texas

Grandpa

The air of the sea preceded him.
He was salt spray lifted from waves
   by winds that carried the scent of spice
        from exotic lands.

He would bring fresh fish
   and oysters.
   Sometimes wild duck
     would grace our table.

      And, always, stories of how he got them.

I remember days on the beach
walking with him,
     finding treasures that had been lost
         by some sailor's misfortune.

The fall of evening would light his hair.
He was sunset over Galveston Bay.
  He was excitement of dolphins
       running before the ferry.

A carpenter's tools hold the imprints
of strong hands and long use.
The tools of a man who built churches
   and a house to hold his family.

Rosewood and brass…
    now, I use them.

Some people say he was a hard man.
   A stubborn old Scot
   who had to have his way.

I prefer my memories of Grandpa.

Beachcombing

Salt air and spice
and the gentle weariness
of a well-worn day
give meaning
where none
is needed.

Pelicans and shearwaters
ride a road found
light above the waves
and gulls tell stories
of loneliness
on the sea.

Treasures hidden beneath
Sargassum and driftwood
allude to mysteries
of their origins
with voices whispering
in wind and sand.

Clues to life's secrets
locked in spirals and fans
and colors of shells
present an amazing gift
with every step
discovery.

Save the Paper.

They were wonderful times,
those holidays now gone,
when we'd gather at home
and laugh with each other.

I look back and wonder
how my parents did it.
They gave to us so much
when they had so little.

As I became a man,
I came to understand
the answer's hiding place…
"Save the paper".

That unassuming phrase
told how they would not waste,
even wrapping paper,
in saving for next year

Each year they did their best,
and their best was enough
to give cherished mem'ries
of growing up with love.

Now my family gathers
around a lighted tree
and love is still flowing
across time and mem'ries.

Not knowing the reason,
often they will shout out
a lovely little phrase…
"Save the paper".

Deer River Farewell

When the leaves begin to fall...
golden fairies dancing their last...
time to leave Deer River again.

We begin to put away
boat docks and the toys of the lake
and feel winter's breath more each day.

The campfire conversations
dwindle and then become quiet...
the words falling into the flames.

I see the eyes of good friends
and I hope they see me as same...
soon, we leave Deer River again.

The kayaks are stored with care
and the folding chairs put away…
the days now, quickly, counting down.

We pack each thing in its place...
carefully each space is thus filled...
then, we just stuff it all away.

The falling leaves will softly
cover the season's memories...
and, we leave Deer River again

A Barr'd Owl moans his farewell
and loons mourn the end of summer.
Chipmunks storing what food they can.

Snows will come and cover all
and the cold will enforce its reign.
Our little place will wait for us.

We will be there, my sweet friends...
when winter has come to its end...
yes, back to Deer River again.

Grendel's Child

The child of Grendel wandered beside the northern sea,
then turned her face from whale-roads to seek the lore of
 Hrothgar's time.
In cold, dark forests that guarded their secrets well, she strode
until she found a moss laden ruin… the place of Grendel's doom.

The graven stone and runic beams of a once great hall
made eldritch claim to the moon's faint light.
Each worm-eaten word carved in graying oak was a trace
of the time when her father walked the fens and moors.

The ashes of fire-pits that had blazed when men sang
the lays of heroes and of their fearsome foes
were cold and wet under the silence of the years.
Yet, she scratched at the dead embers and tried to taste the words.

The crumbling stones and rotting logs of the mead-hall
whispered their secrets in the tongues of rain and wind.
But their thoughts were lost to her and she moved on,
seeking answers that were as the smoke of their fires.

Grendel's child withdrew from the ruin and spat the ash-words.
For it was men who wrote their heroes' tales
and it was they who told of their foes' ill deeds.
No songs of the hall would name them as the monsters they
   could be.

She sat alone, facing the last image of the ancient king
to study the face of he who bartered her father's death.
How else could she yet come to know her father's life
when all who knew him and feared him were now dead?

She lay before the tomb of the Northlander chief
and slumbered through the passing of snows
until the final vestige of Hrothgar passed from this Earth
and the child of Grendel had turned to stone.

Calypso's Children

I hear them.
Some giggle and flirt
with dark eyes half hidden
behind fans of Spanish lace.
Some don't even pretend.
They are consumed by lust.
I walk through them and
my coat sleeve brushes
against their backs.
I feel them
clutching at my clothes.
There are those pure of spirit
who have set lofty goals
and here they compete
with songs of whales,
curses of sailors,
and banshee cries.

Witches are burned,
children are born,
and angels fly 'round and 'round
singing to Ahab and
cigarette girls.
Primal screams and
lovers' vows
wash over bedrock and poets…
eroding science
with the power of myth
and destroying fantasies
with logic's hammer.
They all want me to stop.
To stay a while.
To lay open their secrets.
I don't have enough time
for all of them.
I can only listen to them
pleading from the stacks
of a darkened library.

The End of a Song

A song has ended.
Its echoes fade into mists
and soft answers
from the lake forest.

As long as the lake is there,
and loons remind us
to look into our hearts,
we will hear the song again.

CWO 3 Richard E Byrd

Hero

I heard you were a hero.
That's what someone said;
but, I knew that already.

When we were kids
we played and fought
and had good times.

You defended the helpless:
like the girl in your class
the teacher had wronged.

The Marines came next
and so you found
a brotherhood there.

The merciless fires of war
tempered your character
but did not harden your soul.

Four sons and a daughter
you raised with love…
and the love grew in them.

If it is love of family
that gives immortality
so you are remembered.

I heard you were a hero.
That's what someone said;
but, we knew that already.

Huey Rider

>We spoke of the days in green heat…
>the times we knew
>before we knew
>each other.
>
>The strength of youth carried us then…
>we did not know
>how years would roll
>over us.
>
>We could laugh and talk of those times…
>and hold at bay
>the deeper thoughts
>haunting us.
>
>All hospitals smell just the same…
>That was the last
>visit we had…
>then I left.
>
>The Agent had taken its toll…
>and crept into
>your body's cells
>and took you.
>
>Hey, maybe we will meet again…
>I'll jump on board.
>Thanks for the ride,
>Door Gunner.

In Green Fields

In green fields the soldiers lay,
their dreams now enriching dirt.
How did they come to their last day?

The flags did wave and bands did play.
They were so bright, so young, and alert.
People cheered them along their way.

They heard what their leaders had to say;
medals would be on every shirt,
they would be victors, come what may.

They weren't told how Death collects his pay.
How he would follow the pain and the hurt …
how some would beg him to take them away.

They would act the parts in the devil's play
as the drums of war began their cruel concert
in flashes and poundings and splashes of clay.

Without regret they send our youth away;
those leaders who lie and truth subvert.
So, this is how they met their final day…
sightless eyes staring at the sun's last ray.

Veterans' Day

They are all around you
and you are unaware.
They are our mothers and fathers...
uncles and aunts.
Sisters and Brothers.

She watches her children
breathing softly in sleep
Then she cries for other babies
who will not wake.
Girls and boys in a sad land
where playgrounds erupt
in spiteful flames.

He teaches your sons
and your daughters...
or, maybe, he works
on your car while you wait
and you are not aware
that he remembers chaos
for a little while
each, and every, day.

Another finds his way past cold eyes;
through streets that have…
become indifferent.
His only friend will be a bottle,
or a small tube of glass,
that will help him forget
battles he cannot control.

Sometimes they seem far away…
with eyes watching
a distant place.
Be patient…
You cannot see those
who are standing beside them.
You don't see the faces
of friends that sleep
in gardens of stone.

Some find it easier to condemn them
rather than try to understand,
that the memories they cannot escape
are as close as yesterday morning.
And there are battles
to be fought
each day.

The Homecoming

After you have been through the fiery nights
and have had to face uncertain dawns
there comes the time when you return home.

It doesn't seem the same any more,
the streets are not as long as they were before
and the houses are so much smaller.

The people you knew still rake their leaves
and cut their lawns as they have always done…
but somehow it is not the same.

Friends call out to you and invite you in.
You all gather at the same old bar
but they seem louder now; child-like… and innocent.

You let their happy noise babble around you…
and you realize that their tides and streams
are no longer the currents that carry you.

As you get up to leave, you see another,
whose eyes tell you that they have seen the same.
You both move to a table, away from the noise, and drink.

Neither says much… just a place name in a strange tongue.
Then both nod and drink the beer and think back
 to all the days you spent in Hell.

It is then, in such a bittersweet time,
when you learn that home has not changed.
No, they have not changed… you have.

Damned Strange

I heard them beating their damned drums.
they pounded out senseless,
random rhythms,
  banging   and   banging
    all night
  to scare away any forest demons
    waiting to steal their souls
        when we killed them.

Nobody told us if the demons
would be after our souls.

Maybe said vile spirits
would not consider us
       worthwhile.

Maybe the drum banging
would protect us, too.

If so, we owed the Viet Cong
a word of thanks.
    If not, they just cost us a little sleep.
At about three in the morning,
the drums went silent.
They would be crossing the river
and we would be stopping them.

Huey

We knew the sound they made
   when they were coming in.
The rattle and roar of blades
   whipping the sky.

  Then
    Whop whop whop whop
when they swooped down to pick us up.

We would climb on board,
  bone-aching tired,
    with our wounded
    with our dead.
And they would rise out of the dust
   and the stink
   into clean air
   unburdened by heat
   and bugs
   and land mines
   and punji pits.

Now they fly in our memories
   and we know that,
   when it comes time
     to lift us up,
We will not be waiting
   for chariots
   or angel hosts…

It will be a Huey
  that comes to take us home.

The Missing One

One is missing.
It has happened before.
The hunt begins and
all the likely places
are searched through
and again… and again.
The other, whose mate is gone,
is now apart
from the community,
no longer a part of the rest.
From time to time
the same places
are searched anew, but,
one is still missing.
They, like geese,
are together for life.
Its mate lingers on for a while
until it is time for it to go.
All the others do not notice
its passing.
Was it some tiny Rapture
that took the one away?
Did it slip, unknowing,
into some inter-dimensional
realm from which
it will never return?
Are there parallel universes
where it and its mate
are still together?
Did Bigfoot get it?
Where *is* that sock?

Carnival

Riding a bright-lighted wheel of ups and downs
going 'round and around, in a circle of clowns.

Ever more flashing, the bright costumes they wear
each hiding the burdens of truth that they bear.

They have painted their faces with smiles and grins
that gloss over the pain of knowing their sins.

Torch-light dancing on a gaudy canvas world
that gives empty promises each time unfurled.

They go chasing the paper that buys their toys
and begin to ignore the source of their joys.

Posing on pedestals of profit and whim
that won't bear their weight when the spotlight goes dim.

So. when they bow out at the end of their time,
they will have played the role of a handcuff'd mime.

Around and around in a circle of clowns.

A Family Album at Christmas

A small child and an old man with the same face,
Time and the turn of a page keep them in place.

There are faces of those we don't remember,
but they still return to us each December.

We visit them again as we decorate
and put out the stockings and the festive plate.

Children ask us to read out a fading name…
who all these people were, and from where they came.

It's in this season of memorable times
when we look at this book of eloquent mimes

knowing the names will be forgotten one day
and the photographs will slowly fade away.

Yet, the ties from our ancestors are still there…
in the color of eyes or curling of hair.

They are us… always… we will remember that.

Swamp Water

Swamp water moves.
It holds life
and
it holds death.
It ripples with secrets
from dim ages
that
creep out from
cold, reptilian brains
hiding deep in
dark
swamp water.

Ivy

I put the little ivy plant out to die.
It did not fare well in the window.
Placing it on a bench by the old wooden fence,
I thought it would enjoy fall's last sun
before winter ended its struggle.

The frosts came and exacted their toll
as plants around the ivy gave up their colors.
Leaves fell and winter came to claim it's due.
Yet, small green leaves still peeked from the pot
beneath a hood of freezing white.

Winter surrendered to spring's hope
and plants rejoiced in the warming sun.
There was much activity for them to do.
They had to grow and show their glory again.
Amid it all, small green leaves still peeked from the pot.

They grew slowly and hung over the edge.
The pot disappeared beneath the green hope
of a living thing's desire to be what it is.
It fought back at the summer's heat
and withstood the dry time that came with it.

I marveled at this small green fighter.
That bench was to be where it met its fate,
but its fate was not what I expected.
It had become a place of resurrection.
A teaching place to school me in life's tenacity.

The cold returned and the sun lowered in the sky.
But, there was more than just a little bit of green.
The ivy's tendrils had spread on the top of the bench.
It was showing the world what it was to become
and it was prepared for the winter's fast.

It has now grown to cover much of the fence
and spread out a little on the ground.
It hangs there in quiet dignity, its leaves waving,
and it tells me, without reproach, it belongs here
and so, do I.

Deer River Flow

Spirit Walk

Feel rain on your face, smell the freshening air.
Cold wind rising, pulling and ruffling your hair.
The sky colors form an arch into the lake
and it speaks of a time we had to forsake.

Fish are still biting, so you cast out again,
then you hear a call, from your soul's deepest plain.
The old one is calling you, and you listen.
Colors in the water sparkle and glisten.

The ancient one in you returning with joy…
the wild one you let run when you were a boy.
He feels the sleet biting into your quick grin
and you want to run with him through brae and fen.

He is the one who kept the way of the fang,
who knew how to sing until the mountains rang.
The one who remembers old spirits' faces
when the streams and forests were sacred places.

Return to the forests, return to the wild.
To places that whispered when you were a child,
that told of brother wolves running in wild chases
in that long time before men became races.

Smell the sweet juniper and the Earth's good loam.
Listen for the loon's call where the moose still roam.
Run before the storm and run before the rain,
Run with the spirit of the old one again.

When you have found the place our souls remember,
go to the fire pit to find the last ember.
She is the dream maker, the mother of flames,
she listened when your ancestors spoke their names.

Bring her offerings of tinder and lighter,
old memories to ignite and burn brighter.
She is the dream maker, you ask her the way,
and you begin your spirit walk on that day.

On Deer River Flow

I went to where a rainbow touched the shore
and I found no pot of gold lying there.
A zephyr made ferns share their ancient lore
but I did not ken their language fair.

Great trees also told of good things to know
about slow lives under the soaring eaves,
about what they dream under winter's snow,
and how sunlight dances through playful leaves.

Gray rocks accepted the afternoon sun
and gave themselves to mosses and flowers,
providing the chipmunks a place to run
and hide from the early spring showers.

Often, I think, our lives become so poor
when we forget to value Nature's share.
I went to where a rainbow touched the shore
and so I found the treasures waiting there.

Sing, Wounded Soul

I cannot hold your cries,
they slip through my fingers.
I cannot take away your pain,
it lies so far beyond my reach.
I cannot dig out your sorrow,
its roots are too deep.
I cannot chase away your fears,
They hide and creep out later.
I can only tell you, you are loved.
So, sing, wounded soul…
your tears do not fall into emptiness.

Critical Mass

There once was a little man who didn't like anybody.
He folded himself up into a tiny wad of hate.
The gravity of his brooding discontent
sent him spiraling ever inward
and he became a singularity
of himself and his woes
no one knew until
he was
gone

.

Cirque du Soleil

You removed me from my worries
      and carried me into your magical land.
You lifted my burdens and returned
      memories of youth.
You erased a little of the cynicism born in war
      reminding me of the beauty to be found
      in the talents of all peoples.
You took me, for a while,
   from the aches and fears of being old
      and taught me how to fly.

Totems

A man touches a fallen giant
and his spirit whispers to it.
He gives new meaning
to the death of a tree.

Blades and patience are the tools
bringing forth the forms
that sleep within the wood.
Shavings fall and creatures grow.

Water and earth and air
and that which is unseen
have given the giant its mass.
Now some returns and some remains.

By talent and care creatures form…
each in its domain
honoring all that live
in the world the giant portrays.

The fish is at the bottom
where the waters flow.
The water is a blessing to all
and all depend on it.

Next is the turtle
bridging water and land.
Land and water together
give rise to forest and grasses.

The snake has no way to walk,
yet traverses water and land…
teaching us we can overcome
difficult ways and troubles.

Over the snake of the land,
a raccoon climbs for the sky,
It is a creature of the land
yet it strives to reach higher.

An eagle soars above them,
a lord of the sky.
Its clear eyes see far
as it surveys water, land, and forest.

Watching over them
is the eye of God.
These beings are of His heart
and He loves them all.

The eye of God also watches
the totem that is not there.
The totem that is missing
from the rising tower of symbols.

That totem can destroy the rest
if it does not care,
or it can save them all
if wisdom is its share.

The missing totem touches a fallen giant
and his spirit whispers to it.

Two Women by the Sea

I saw two women by the surf
scattering ashes to the waves.
They stood and faced the great salt sea
and each then leaned to hold the other.

Standing against the easterly winds,
they stolidly faced this last farewell
and tears fell to sweeten the foam
with memories of yesterday's love.

But the tide had turned in sad retreat
and the water refused the offering.
They dug at the sand with shells and hands
to send the soul to the sea with love.

This was to be their last sweet touch…
the last caress of one so cherished.
They scraped and worked with what they had
And I knew their tears were falling.

I walked, as fast as old legs would carry,
back to my truck to get my shovel.
But when I returned, the women were gone
and so, I hoped, was the one they loved.

                              New Smyrna Beach
                              Florida

Cricket

Carrier of the wolf's code.
Brave little heart…
five pounds of hair and happiness.
Defending your family,
attacking that large dog,
your strategy was to jump
down its throat and...
choke it to death.
Well, you made it half way.
The stitches did not quell
that great spirit for long.
Soon you were back
to your scratch and sniff,
jump for joy
happy dog
self.

Cricket Wolfbane, Dog of Dogs,
you were my sweet little friend
for seventeen years.

Laws

First Law

Energy and matter
cannot be created,
cannot be destroyed.
You can only change their forms.
There is no more.
There is no less.
This is all there is.
    So,
You must accept it…

    Until you laugh
or hear a song.
Until you fall in love
or hold your child.
The First Law
    is of physics,
the rest is of the spirit.

Second Law

Energy flows toward entropy.
        ...or...
    Things run down.
Then, life blooms,
   jumps,
      slithers,
         hops,
            into the equation
It is order, on an inconceivable scale,
rising from chaos.
    Yes,
the individual being succumbs to
    the Second Law.
But, life itself fights to repudiate it.
    Eventually,
the Second Law will win.
    Maybe.
        See: parallel universe.

Deer River Flow

Dawn of a Lesser Light

Low-flying geese send their cries skipping across the night.
    Flat stones of sound fading,
        then sinking into the lake.

A heron waits near the shore
        and I watch it hold its ancient duty.
            We wait for the first glimmer
        beyond the mountains…
the heron to better see silver flashes
        slipping through the shallows,
            and I to wonder
                at the light of our pale sister.
The heron's voice croaks out an echo
        from its saurian past
            telling me the history of its tribe.
And I gather dim memories from colder ages.
                Old memories hiding within me.
Memories of herons and men
        ever waiting
            for the rising of the moon.

Under the Wizard's Hat

Sitting with Michaela under the wizard's hat
Watching the crystal points sewn in the night's cloak
When the moon plays shy
And waits to tease the morning.

Little ghosts from ethereal coldness
Streak their brief souls across spangled velvet.
Our eyes drink in the wonder,
Our minds explore the universe.

Katydids and Katydidn'ts sing their arguments
For the benefit of all who care.
And we listen to their ancient chorus.
Sitting with Michaela under the wizard's hat.

Tranquil Summer Memories

I remember when life was carefree and simple.
    With lazy days and endless play hours.
I remember hot days, cooling off with a quick swim,
    And the cool sensation of water
    Flowing through my fingers.
I remember warm summer rainstorms, with the
    Gentle pitter-patter of raindrops on
    The roof.
I remember the fresh smell of grass after mowing,
    And walking barefoot while the cool
    Grass blades tickled my toes.
I remember fireflies glowing in the night sky,
    Like fireworks on the fourth of July.
    And cool summer nights lying beneath
    The stars while the katydids sang a
    Sweet lullaby.
I remember falling asleep embraced by my hammock,
    And my Daddy picking me up, putting me
    In my warm bed, and kissing me goodnight.

                        Michaela Nicole Ethridge
                        Father's Day 1999

Winter's Clear Light

Table cloth flowers etched clean
by sun off the white of snow.
Coffee steams its promise
and wakens awareness in each breath.

Memory's march made bold
by aromas of bacon and eggs
take thoughts home again
to where the heart is happiest.

I hold the warmth of a cup
in grateful, aging hands
lit by winter's clear light.

Words From the River

They sleep near a great river
and, perhaps, dream of flowing water.
We gave them a gray stone
with a short story etched on it.
A few words to carry a lifetime;
to tell of love and children;
of disappointments and triumphs;
of struggles and strengths.
The sun and rain will someday
do their work and erase it all.
But, the river will still be there...
marking the passing of the seasons.
Someday the river will change its path.
Maybe, in some coming age,
it will be here...
and it will take them
to rest in the sea.
For now, I will stand by this stone
and listen to words from the river.

           For William Carlton Byrd
                  and
              Bernice Ina Byrd

Deer River Flow

In the Glowing of Fall

I want to be with you when the red leaves fall,
when the frost returns and the high geese call.
When the spring has passed with its innocent ways
and memories now hold our warm, summer days.

I want to share a fire when stars sting the night
and the dark hills hide all else from our sight.
When, with soft tyranny, smoke demands our tears
and we remember other nights, fires, and years.

I want to hold your hands and warm them in mine
as I drink, with you, the last of life's sweet wine.
I want to be with you in the glowing of Fall;
when the frost is here and the last geese call.

At Winter's End

I want to be with you
as wind passes through the trees…
and the rain falls lightly
like tears onto the earth.

I want to be with you
when our work here is done…
and our hearts beat no more
for others to hear.

I want to be with you
as we pass through Death's gate…
into the light
of eternal peace.

I want to be with you
as forever becomes part of our existence…
and we live only
in others' memories.

I want to be with you
at winter's end…
When we walk on God's shore
hand in hand as the lovers we've always been

                              Kathryn Grace Byrd
                              June, 2008

Haiku

Novice

A poor example,
this haiku haltingly made,
my first attempted.

 Then, someone reminded me that haiku normally deals with nature in some way. Therefore, I wrote my second haiku.

Got it Right

Ordinarily,
haiku is of nature's realm;
so, I add a leaf.

Seasons

Cycle

A leaf has fallen.
It graces the forest floor…
a gift of essence.

Renewal

Raindrops on old wood
awaken the sleeping ones.
Spring, smiling, returns.

Essence

Summer spirit comes
drifting in a welcome breeze.
The scent of hot pine.

Oracles

Summer memories
drift softly in autumn's breath
forewarning of snow.

Promises

Snow on the firewood…
hiding the warm promises
of the fire within.

Explanations and Inspirations

Siren Borealis

A little south of Malone, New York, there flows a beautiful little river. It is called Deer River. At a place just inside the Adirondack Park, there is a campground, Deer River Campground, where my wife and I like to spend our summers.

The moon rising over De Bars Mountain and reflecting on the water of Deer River Flow inspired this poem. The night was cold and the north wind whispered through the trees. Borealis not only means "of the north", it also means "of the north wind".

A Poet Speaks

This was written while listening to the poet, Dr. Katie Chapel (University of West Georgia), read her powerful and beautiful work.

Coffee

Anyone who enjoys a hot cup of coffee knows the reason I wrote this.

One Step Down

One Step Down was one of my favorite hang-outs when I was in the Army. I would go there and listen to some fine Jazz. When I returned in 2007, I was disappointed to see the door covered with plywood and a small notice pasted over it.

Short List

Written after a cold, wet, delightful day with some Canadian friends at Deer River Campsite. I wanted to write something as undemanding and straight-forward as those good friends.

An Unfortunate Word

A friend wrote a poem about the word yes. I decided to write one about no.

Photographs by a Balcony Window

My dear friend, Dina Televitskaya sent me photographs of herself, Vladimir, and their cat, Peach, on their balcony in St. Petersburg, Russia.

Concerning the Converse of Eagles and Men

There is a man, Oakley, who seems to have been given the trust of animals. Once, he was out on Deer River Flow when a fawn left its mother on shore, swam to his boat, and tried to climb on board. He had to keep pushing the fawn away with an oar until it finally returned to its mother. He was not being cruel; because, he thought if he touched it his scent might make the doe reject the fawn. Sometimes, when Oakley catches a fish, he will hold it up and an American Bald Eagle will come down to land on his boat and accept his gift.

You must understand that, in this poem, I am not inferring that Oakley is less than truthful. I am merely observing the common sin of many fishermen... I being one of them... mea culpa.

Fish Tale

The reason for this poem is obvious.

Barnyard Bully

I had a rooster that would attack anyone entering the chicken pen. One day he just keeled over and died. I think it was from pure meanness.

For Your Mother and Mine

For Your Mother and Mine was written to honor my mother and the mother of Dina Televitskaya. Although they were from such different places, they were both strong women and would probably have been good friends. It was read at my amazing mother's funeral.

Grandpa
Ekphrastic poetry written after observing a painting. quillandparchment.com

Beachcombing
Remembering Galveston, Bolivar Peninsula, and the adventures of a boy growing up on
the Texas Gulf Coast.

Save the Paper
My grandmother and my parents survived the Great Depression. They had to learn how to save everything and make their money last as long as possible. As my brothers, my sister and I were growing up; we would hear the same phrase every Christmas: "Save the paper." I think we had one roll of wrapping paper that must lasted ten years. Even though we are not, now, in as lean times, I still say "save the paper" each Christmas… more as a remembrance of my parents and grandmother than for the sake of a few scraps of paper. Now, my children and my grandchildren have taken up the phrase.

Deer River Farewell
Near the beginning of October, as the weather cools, everyone in Deer River Campsite must start the process of closing their places for the coming winter. Packing things away and leaving Deer River Flow is always a little sad.

Grendel's Child
One of the campers at Deer River Campsite carved a
bearded man's head in an old stump. It was eventually moved to a place in the forest just off the drive. It has become covered with moss and is a beautiful part of the setting. While sitting and pondering it, I first started writing a poem about Hrothgar, the king who hired Beowulf to slay Grendel; but, the large stone in the foreground kept demanding my attention… (look closely at the rock in the foreground of the picture, you will see her)… Grendel's Child was the result.

Calypso's Children
Walking through a storage/workroom in Neva Lomason Memorial Library in Carrollton, Georgia, I could almost hear the books in the stacks whispering to me. Yeah, I know, I let my imagination run away with me sometimes.

The End of a Song
My friend Guy was a musician. There were times when he would sit at his keyboard and play for us. His songs would ring out across Deer River Flow.

Hero
While at Deer River, I learned of the death of my brother, Richard E. Byrd. Eddie was a career Marine who retired as a Chief Warrant Officer. He and I were both in Vietnam at the same time. One of my friends there told me of a conversation he had had with a Marine. He had mentioned that my brother was a Marine and gave his name. The Marine replied, "You mean Sgt. Richard E. Byrd, the hero?"

I miss him.

Huey Rider
Dave Donaldson was a friend at Deer River. He, also, was a Vietnam veteran. We both knew the strange mix of hate/love emotions concerning the Huey helicopter. The machine could be a beast carrying you into a bad situation and it could be an angel's chariot flying in to save you. I think most veterans of that conflict have similar feelings about the Huey.
Dave had been a door gunner on a Huey. He worked with too much Agent Orange, a defoliant, during his tour of duty.

In Green Fields
I just wanted to write a villanelle.

Veterans' Day
I was talking to an elementary teacher and did not know that he, too, was a war veteran (Desert Storm).

The Homecoming
On thinking about the feelings I experienced after returning home from Vietnam.

Damned Strange
Memories of a strange night in 1966

Huey
I watched a history program about helicopters. It brought back memories of the Bell UH-1 Iroquois. The Huey

The Missing One
While attending a meeting of the Georgia Poetry Society, I listened to Thomas Lux reading some of his work during a workshop. A line from one of his poems provided the seed that grew into this poem. Many times a word, or phrase, from the work of someone else strikes a spark in your mind that grows into something new.

Carnival
Yearly, around the last of July, I meet with several writers from around the country at the Glenmore Inn on Big Moose Lake. If you are interested, it is the place from which Chester Gillette and Grace Brown left to go on their fateful boat ride. Gillette allegedly murdered Grace on Big Moose Lake and was subsequently convicted and executed for the crime. Theodore Dreiser later wrote *An American Tragedy* based on that event.
I digress, some of the other writers and I came up with a poetic form which we called a Tamarack. It was modeled after the structure of a Tamarack branch. *Carnival* is a poem written in that form.

A Family Album at Christmas
    I like to write a poem to put in with Christmas cards each year. This one is also in the Tamarack form.

Swamp Water
    When I was young, I lived in Beaumont, Texas. Near Beaumont are some beautiful swamps and bayous. My friends and I had some wonderful times hunting, fishing, and camping there. *Swamp Water* was written in the form of poetry called Shape, wherein the poem takes the shape of the subject. In this case, a reflection in the slow ripples of swamp water.

Ivy
    A small ivy growing in a flower pot in the kitchen window seemed to be always struggling to survive there. It had plenty of sunlight and the right amount of water, but it just didn't look healthy. I finally gave up on the little ivy plant… it did not give up on me.

Spirit Walk
    It was a cold day in May when this photograph was taken. I put the camera away and continued fishing. The temperature

dropped and sleet moved in. *Spirit Walk* began to form.

On Deer River Flow
    While kayaking across Deer River Flow, I decided to go to the point where a rainbow (picture on the page facing Spirit Walk) seemed to touch the shore. I enjoyed the surroundings and some berries, *On Deer River Flow* was the result.

Sing, Wounded Soul
    This was written for my Russian friend, Dina Televitskaya and her husband Vladimir Mehailov who live in St. Petersburg. It was published in a book of her poetry "It Is Necessary to Live".
    I like to read this poem each time I am asked to present

my work at some gathering. Many people have come to me to say how much it helped them. I say this, not out of conceit, but because I believe I was merely the vessel that held these words until they could be written.

If you know of someone who might find comfort in this poem, you may copy it and give it to them.

Critical Mass
A televised program about the universe made me think of how people can sometimes implode spiritually and emotionally to become a Black Hole of their own inner space

Cirque du Soleil
They put on an incredible show.

Totems
One day at Deer River I sat and watched John Safford working at a log with his chisels. He is a quiet man (with a poet hiding inside him) who rides a Harley with his wife, Suzie.

Two Women by the Sea
Sadness on a Florida beach.

Cricket
We had a Yorkshire Terrier who possessed a great heart and a wonderful spirit.

Laws
While waiting in the car and working a crossword puzzle, I was listening to Un Bel Di from Madame Butterfly and I came upon the word entropy. As I stared at that word, Kiri Te Kanawa started singing that beautiful passage with the massed strings behind her (you know the one, and if you don't, you need to look it up).

Dawn of a Lesser Light
Sitting quietly, watching a heron, and waiting for moonrise.

Under the Wizard's Hat and **Tranquil Summer Memories**
When my daughter, Michaela, was small, we would spend time together looking at the night sky. I wrote *Under the Wizard's Hat* for her. The Georgia summer nights were warm and the katydids were talented.

I have included a poem, *Tranquil Summer Memories,* Michaela wrote for me as a Father's Day gift. I thought you might like it... I certainly do.

Winter's Clear Light
Waiting for breakfast in the home of Linda and Loren Taylor of Nicholville, New York, I looked at my hands and saw my father's hands. The sunlight coming off the snow outside lit the table with that beautiful, crisp winter light.

Words From the River
On our way home to Georgia, after I had read some of my work to the Vermont House of Representatives, my wife and I were stranded in New Jersey by transmission problems and a storm. The flooding and destruction in the wake of the storm delayed the delivery of a new transmission and shut down the airport for several days. While we were there, I was informed of my mother's death. We were, therefore, unable to get to Texas for her funeral.

I know the place where my parents are buried. The

Neches River flows nearby within sight. There are beautiful old trees with Spanish moss moving in the gentle breeze. I wrote this for my mother and father. As I said in the introduction, the words, *Words From the River,* had their own idea where they belonged.

In the Glowing of Fall
Written for my sweet wife, Kathy.

At Winter's End

In the poem at the beginning of this book, one of the lines I had written was "Words drift from dream's realm". The poem *At Winter's End* came to Kathy in a dream while at Deer River. She had to write it quickly before it faded away as dreams often do. It is the only poem she has written.

Previous Publishers

Above Ground Testing

    Rainy Day Riff

Bang (Duewest Publishing)

    Sing, Wounded Soul

Cradle Songs: An Anthology of Poems on Motherhood

    For Your Mother and Mine

It is Necessary to Live (Poetry by Dina Televitskaya, St. Petersburg, Russia)

    Sing, Wounded Soul

Poetry Soup (poetrysoup.com)

    Concerning the Converse of Eagles and Men
    Novice
    Got it Right
    Cycle
    Oracles

Quill and Parchment (quill and parchment.com)

    A poem's Way
    A Poet Speaks
    Bouquet
    Dawn of a Lesser Light
    Grandpa
    Grendel's Child
    In the Glowing of Fall
    One Step Down

Reach of Song (Georgia Poetry Society Anthology)

Grendel's Child

www.ingramcontent.com/pod-product-compliance
Lightning Source LLC
Chambersburg PA
CBHW052113070526
44584CB00017B/2470